# LIVING FROM THE SOUL

# LIVING *from the* SOUL

## THE 7 SPIRITUAL PRINCIPLES
### *of* RALPH WALDO EMERSON

THE SECRET OF LIFE IS THE SOUL.

WRITTEN BY
**Sam Torode**

ILLUSTRATED BY
**Alexander Marchand**

# CONTENTS

# EMERSON AT SEA

WHAT DO YOU DO WHEN YOUR WORLD **FALLS APART**? WHERE CAN YOU FIND **PEACE** IN THE MIDST OF **UNCERTAINTY**? WHO CAN YOU TURN TO FOR **GUIDANCE**?

THESE ARE AMONG THE QUESTIONS I FACED AT THE AGE OF THIRTY.

MY BELOVED WIFE **ELLEN** HAD DIED FROM TUBERCULOSIS IN FEBRUARY, 1831, AFTER ONLY EIGHTEEN MONTHS OF MARRIAGE. I WAS A CHRISTIAN MINISTER, LIKE MY FATHER AND GRANDFATHER BEFORE HIM. BUT IN THE MONTHS AFTER ELLEN'S DEATH, MY BELIEFS BEGAN TO **CHANGE**, DIVERGING FROM TRADITIONAL CHRISTIANITY. NO LONGER COMFORTABLE REPEATING THE RITES AND CREEDS OF THE PAST, I **RESIGNED** FROM THE PASTORATE.

SEPT. 22 1811

FEB. 8 1831

IN DECEMBER, 1832, I WAS AN UNEMPLOYED FORMER MINISTER WITH NO FALLBACK PLAN. SUDDENLY, I DECIDED TO SET **SAIL** FOR EUROPE. NOW I WAS AT SEA—BOTH FIGURATIVELY AND LITERALLY.

DURING MY TEN-MONTH TOUR, I SPENT TIME IN MALTA, ITALY, FRANCE, ENGLAND, AND SCOTLAND.

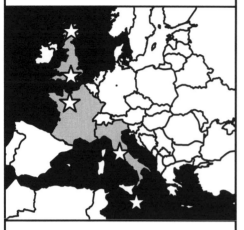

I ATTENDED LECTURES BY THE LEADING SCIENTISTS OF THE DAY AND MET EMINENT AUTHORS INCLUDING SAMUEL TAYLOR COLERIDGE, THOMAS CARLYLE, AND WILLIAM WORDSWORTH.

VISITING THE GARDEN OF PLANTS AND CABINET OF NATURAL HISTORY IN PARIS, I HAD AN **EPIPHANY** OF THE INTERRELATEDNESS OF ALL LIFE. I WROTE IN MY JOURNAL ON THE VOYAGE HOME:

*That which I cannot yet declare has been my angel from childhood until now.*
*It has inspired me with hope. It cannot be defeated with my defeats.*

*It is the glory that shall be revealed; it is the open secret of the universe.*
*I believe in this life.*
*I believe it continues.*
*As long as I am here, I plainly read my duties as writ with a pencil of fire. They speak not of death. They are woven of immortal thread.*

WHAT DID I MEAN BY THIS GUIDING **"ANGEL"**? WHAT WAS THE "OPEN SECRET OF THE UNIVERSE"?

ANSWER:

NOTE: THROUGHOUT THIS BOOK THE SOUL WILL BE REPRESENTED BY THIS RADIATING CIRCLE SYMBOL.

LIKE MOST OF US, I HAD BEEN TAUGHT TO THINK OF THE SOUL AS AN IMMORTAL SPIRIT **PLACED INSIDE** EACH OF US BY **GOD**, WHICH CAN BE EITHER SAVED OR DAMNED. BUT AS MY FAITH EVOLVED DURING THESE TUMULTUOUS YEARS, CULMINATING IN MY PILGRIMAGE ABROAD, I CAME TO A VERY DIFFERENT UNDERSTANDING.

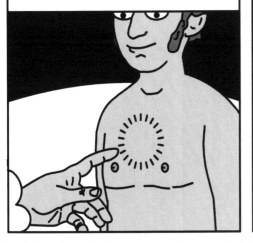

THROUGH MEDITATION AND EXPERIENCE, I CAME TO SEE MY **SOUL** AS A PART OF THE UNIVERSAL CONSCIOUSNESS. THE "OVERSOUL," I CONCLUDED, IS THE VERY GROUND OF EXISTENCE, OUT OF WHICH ALL THINGS—ENERGY, MATTER, LIFE—COME INTO BEING.

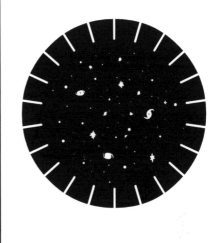

WE CANNOT DEFINE THE SOUL, ONLY EVOKE IT WITH METAPHOR AND POETRY. IT IS LIKE THE **SUN**—TOO BRIGHT TO BE GAZED UPON DIRECTLY, YET BY IT WE SEE ALL THINGS. PICTURE A VAST OCEAN, WITH OUR INDIVIDUAL SOULS BEING WAVES UPON IT, EMERGING FOR A TIME AND THEN RETURNING TO THE WHOLE.

INDIVIDUALITY IS SECONDARY TO **UNITY**. EACH OF US IS **INSEPARABLE** FROM ALL PEOPLE, ALL PLANTS AND ANIMALS, THE EARTH, OUR SOLAR SYSTEM, AND THE ENTIRE COSMOS. AND WE EACH CARRY THE UNIVERSE INSIDE OURSELVES, JUST AS EACH WAVE CARRIES THE OCEAN.

3

THE SOUL CANNOT BE INTELLECTUALLY GRASPED OR SCIENTIFICALLY EXAMINED; IT CAN ONLY BE FELT, LOVED, AND ENJOYED. THROUGH OUR INDIVIDUAL SOULS, WE HAVE DIRECT ACCESS TO THE **UNIVERSAL SOUL—GOD.**

THIS IS NOT A PIPE

THIS IS NOT A SOUL...
JUST A REPRESENTATION

FOR THIS REASON "GOD MUST BE SOUGHT **WITHIN**, NOT WITHOUT." RELIGIOUS INSTITUTIONS AND AUTHORITIES, AT THEIR BEST, CAN ONLY SERVE AS SIGNPOSTS TO A PERSONAL COMMUNION WITH THE DIVINE. AT THEIR WORST, THEY ARE OBSTACLES THAT KEEP US FROM FINDING AND FOLLOWING OUR OWN INNER LIGHT.

THERE ARE NO SUCH THINGS AS "LOST SOULS"...ONLY PEOPLE WHO HAVE FORGOTTEN THEIR CONNECTION TO SOUL. AND THAT CONNECTION CAN BE REDISCOVERED AND NURTURED BY **LOOKING WITHIN.**

UPON MY RETURN, I SETTLED OUTSIDE BOSTON IN THE SMALL TOWN OF **CONCORD**, WHERE I WOULD LIVE FOR THE REST OF MY LIFE. AND I BEGAN A NEW CAREER— LECTURER. DRAWING ON ALL I'D LEARNED IN EUROPE AND ENGLAND, I SPOKE TO EAGER AUDIENCES ABOUT SCIENCE, PHILOSOPHY, AND CULTURE.

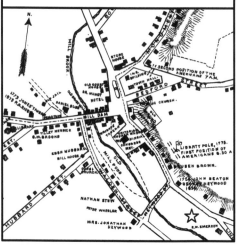

I ALSO BEGAN WRITING A BOOK INSPIRED BY MY **EPIPHANY** IN PARIS. DECADES BEFORE CHARLES DARWIN PUBLISHED ON THE ORIGIN OF SPECIES, I CONCEIVED OF LIFE AS A SINGLE TAPESTRY, WITH THE SIMPLEST FORMS EVOLVING INTO THE MOST COMPLEX. I ENCAPSULATED THIS VISION IN THE EPIGRAPH OF MY FIRST BOOK, **NATURE** (1836):

A SUBTLE CHAIN OF COUNTLESS RINGS THE NEXT UNTO THE FARTHEST BRINGS; THE EYE READS OMENS WHERE IT GOES, AND SPEAKS ALL LANGUAGES THE ROSE; AND, STRIVING TO BE MAN, THE WORM MOUNTS THROUGH ALL THE SPIRES OF FORM.

UNLIKE DARWIN, HOWEVER, I SAW NATURE AS THE MANIFESTATION OF **SPIRIT**. THE UNIVERSAL SOUL IS THE FUNDAMENTAL, ETERNAL REALITY, EXPRESSING ITSELF IN THE REALM OF MATTER AND TIME THROUGH EVER-CHANGING PHYSICAL FORMS.

FOLLOWING MY LIFE TRANSFORMATION, I WAS STILL A PREACHER AT HEART. BUT INSTEAD OF TAKING THE **BIBLE** AS MY STARTING POINT, I PROCLAIMED THE "DIVINE WORD" AS REVEALED IN ALL OF **NATURE** AND **HUMAN CULTURE**.

BUT LET'S RETURN TO SEPTEMBER OF 1833, WHEN I SET OUT FROM LIVERPOOL, BOUND FOR BOSTON. BY DAY, I WALKED THE DECK OF THE SHIP AND GAZED OUT AT THE **VAST SEA**, WHICH SEEMED TO ME A METAPHOR FOR THE OVERSOUL. BY NIGHT, I RECORDED MY INSIGHTS AND EXPLORATIONS IN MY JOURNAL. HAVING BEEN FOR TEN MONTHS IMMERSED IN THE ARTS AND IDEAS OF EUROPE AND ENGLAND, I WAS READY TO STATE MY OWN CONVICTIONS.

5

IN MY JOURNAL ENTRY FOR SEPTEMBER 8, 1833, SHORTLY AFTER EMBARKING, I SPELLED OUT "THE ERROR OF THE RELIGIONISTS"— THOSE WHO CLING TO TRADITION, AUTHORITY, AND DOGMA OF ANY THEOLOGICAL STRIPE: THEY RELY ON **SECONDHAND** REVELATION, WHILE IGNORING OR DERIDING THE SOUL, WHICH IS OUR **DIRECT** CONNECTION TO THE DIVINE.

I THEN ELUCIDATED MY NEW IDEAS—WHICH, I ASSERTED, WERE ACTUALLY SOME OF HUMANITY'S OLDEST INSIGHTS. PARAPHRASED, THESE **SEVEN** CORE PRINCIPLES ARE:

*1. Trust Yourself — All that you need for growth and guidance in life is already present inside you.*

*2. As You Sow, You Will Reap — Your thoughts and actions shape your character, and your character determines your destiny.*

*3. Nothing Outside You Can Harm You — Circumstances and events don't matter as much as what you do with them.*

*4. The Universe Is Inside You — The world around you is a reflection of the world within you.*

*5. Identify with the Infinite — Center your identity on the soul and your life's purpose will unfold.*

*6. Live in the Present — The present moment is your point of power. Eternity is now.*

*7. Seek God Within — The highest revelation is the divinity of the soul.*

THESE WERE THE PRINCIPLES THAT LED ME THROUGH MY DARKEST YEARS AND WOULD CONTINUE TO GUIDE ME TO THE END OF MY DAYS. IN THIS **BRIEF SUMMARY** OF MY PHILOSOPHY, I PROVIDED A TOUCHSTONE FOR MY **ENTIRE** LIFE'S WORK.

# THE IMMENSITY OF THE SOUL

THE MIND SEES, HEARS, LISTENS, SIFTS, WEIGHS, AND DECIDES. BEYOND THIS, THERE IS SOMETHING IN US THAT SEES THE MIND AND WATCHES ITS WORKINGS. THAT SOMETHING IS THE SOUL.
THE SOUL IS THE HIGHEST CONCEPTION OF EXCELLENCE AND TRUTH WE CAN BRING FORTH. AND FROM SEEING WHAT ONE SOUL IS, WE CAN IMAGINE WHAT ALL SOULS MAY BE—AND THUS WE REACH GOD, WHO IS THE UNIVERSAL SOUL.
—ELBERT HUBBARD

MANY PROFESS A BELIEF IN THE SOUL, BUT FEW APPRECIATE ITS IMMENSITY. A SOUL ISN'T SOMETHING THAT YOU HAVE, LIKE AN ARM OR A LEG. IT'S MORE ACCURATE TO SAY THAT **YOUR SOUL HAS YOU**. THE SOUL IS THE VERY GROUND OF YOUR BEING.

THE SOUL ISN'T AN ORGAN LIKE THE HEART OR BRAIN; IT IS THE **POWER** WHICH ANIMATES YOUR ORGANS. IT ISN'T A FUNCTION LIKE MEMORY, CALCULATION, OR COMPARISON; IT IS THE **INTELLIGENCE** WHICH MAKES USE OF THESE FUNCTIONS. IT ISN'T A FACULTY LIKE REASON OR WILLPOWER; IT IS THE **LIGHT** WHICH GUIDES YOUR FACULTIES— IF YOU LET IT.

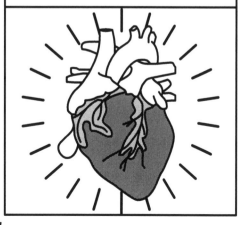

ALL **SIN** CONSISTS IN THINKING AND ACTING AT ODDS WITH THE SOUL. ALL **GOODNESS** CONSISTS IN LETTING THE SOUL EXPRESS ITSELF THROUGH YOU.

THE SOUL SHINES FOR **EVERYONE**. THERE'S A COMMON WISDOM OF HUMANITY SHARED BY ALL PEOPLE, IN ALL PLACES, AT ALL TIMES. THE YOUNG AND THE UNEDUCATED HAVE AS MUCH ACCESS TO THIS WISDOM AS THE OLDEST AND MOST LEARNED.

YOU ARE WISER THAN YOU KNOW. THERE'S A **RESERVOIR OF INSIGHT** WITHIN YOU, JUST WAITING TO BE TAPPED. AWAKEN TO THE IMMENSITY OF THE SOUL, AND IT WILL ILLUMINATE YOUR PATH.

THE LIGHT THAT SHINES ABOVE THE HEAVENS AND ABOVE THIS WORLD, THE LIGHT THAT SHINES IN THE HIGHEST WORLD, BEYOND WHICH THERE ARE NO OTHERS--THAT IS THE LIGHT THAT SHINES IN YOUR HEART.
—THE UPANISHADS

THERE'S A PROFOUND DIFFERENCE BETWEEN FOLLOWING A RELIGION AND LIVING FROM THE SOUL. THOSE WHO RELY ON CHURCH LEADERS, ANCIENT TEXTS, AND OTHER AUTHORITIES FOR GUIDANCE IN LIFE DO NOT REALIZE THE DEPTH AND DEPENDABILITY OF THEIR OWN INNER RESOURCES.

INSTEAD OF CONSULTING THEIR SOUL'S **MORAL COMPASS**, THEY CLING TO RULES AND REGULATIONS PASSED DOWN THROUGH THE AGES, WHICH ARE ALWAYS INCOMPLETE AND IMPERFECT.

WHILE PEOPLE ARGUE OVER WHICH RELIGION HAS THE RIGHT RULES, THE **INFINITE LAW** OF THE UNIVERSE—WHICH GOVERNS EVERYTHING IN EXISTENCE—GOES ON WORKING, SILENT AND UNNOTICED. THIS POWER, WHICH BRINGS ALL THINGS INTO BEING AND GUIDES THEIR DEVELOPMENT, IS IGNORED OR CONSIDERED IRRELEVANT TO THE QUESTIONS WE HUMANS FACE.

ARE WE NOT CHILDREN OF THE UNIVERSE? ARE WE ALONE LEFT WITHOUT GUIDANCE? THE INFINITE LAW LIVES WITHIN IN EACH OF US. IT IS **LIFE ITSELF**. WHEN YOU TURN INWARD AND CONNECT TO THE SOUL, YOU HAVE DIRECT ACCESS TO IT.

IN CHINESE PHILOSOPHY, THE INFINITE LAW IS CALLED THE **TAO** ("THE WAY"). AS LAO TZU DESCRIBES IT, THE TAO CAN BE GLIMPSED BUT NEVER GRASPED. WE MIGHT NAME IT, BUT MUST NEVER CONFUSE A MERE NAME WITH THE REALITY IT REPRESENTS.

THE TAO THAT CAN BE UNDERSTOOD IS NOT THE ETERNAL, COSMIC TAO, JUST AS AN IDEA THAT CAN BE EXPRESSED IN WORDS IS NOT THE INFINITE IDEA. AND YET THIS INEFFABLE TAO IS THE SOURCE OF ALL SPIRIT AND MATTER; EXPRESSING ITSELF, IT IS THE MOTHER OF ALL CREATED THINGS.
—LAO TZU

WE INTUITIVELY DISCERN WHAT IS BEAUTIFUL, GOOD, AND TRUE. OUR **INNER COMPASS** UNFAILINGLY POINTS TO THAT **MAGNETIC NORTH**.

THE REASON YOU ARE DRAWN TO BEAUTY, GOODNESS, AND TRUTH—IN NATURE, ART, AND OTHER PEOPLE—IS BECAUSE THESE QUALITIES **BELONG TO THE SOUL**. THEY WERE ALREADY PRESENT WITHIN YOU BEFORE YOU EVER SAW THEM OUTSIDE YOURSELF. TO THE EXTENT THAT YOU'RE CONNECTED WITH THE SOUL, YOU'LL NATURALLY PURSUE THESE QUALITIES AND DISPLAY THEM IN YOUR LIFE.

YOU MAY BE FOOLED BY OUTWARD APPEARANCES FOR A TIME, BUT IN THE END ONLY THAT WHICH IS TRUE AND GOOD IS RIGHTLY CALLED BEAUTIFUL. BEAUTY, TRUTH AND GOODNESS ARE ULTIMATELY ONE AND THE SAME. THEY ARE DIFFERENT ASPECTS OF **THE ALL**.

WHEN BEAUTY IS ONLY A MASQUERADE, IT IS ACTUALLY UGLINESS. JUST AS GOODNESS, IF IT IS NOT SINCERE, IS NOT REALLY GOODNESS. —LAO TZU

THE WORLD'S RELIGIONS REPRESENT HUMANITY'S ATTEMPTS, IN DIFFERENT TIMES AND PLACES, TO TAKE THE INFINITE LAW OF THE UNIVERSE AND ENCAPSULATE IT IN STORIES AND RITUALS. EACH SECT HOLDS ITS OWN **FRAGMENTARY** VERSION OF THE LAW. BUT IN THE HANDS OF A GENUINE PROPHET OR TEACHER, SECTARIANISM FALLS AWAY AND TRUTH SHINES FORTH IN ALL ITS BEAUTY.

THIS IS WHY, THOUGH THEIR RELIGIONS CONFLICT WITH EACH OTHER ON MANY DOCTRINES, THE GREAT SAINTS OF ALL FAITHS SAY ESSENTIALLY THE **SAME THINGS.** ALL PROCLAIM THE SAME VIRTUES: LOVE, KINDNESS, COURAGE, MODERATION, JUSTICE, DILIGENCE, PATIENCE, MERCY, AND HUMILITY.

IF WE IMAGINE THAT TRUTH HINGES ON THE WORDS OF SOME GREAT TEACHER OR DIVINE BEING, WE WEAKEN ITS POWER. THE DEEPEST TRUTHS ARE **SELF-EVIDENT**; THEY STAND ON THEIR OWN AND NEED NO ARGUMENTS TO PROP THEM UP.

ALL THINGS WHATSOEVER YE WOULD THAT MEN SHOULD DO TO YOU, DO YE SO TO THEM; FOR THIS IS THE LAW AND THE PROPHETS. MATTHEW 7:1

DO NOT DO TO OTHERS WHAT YOU WOULD NOT LIKE YOURSELF. THEN THERE WILL BE NO RESENTMENT AGAINST YOU, EITHER IN THE FAMILY OR IN THE STATE. ANALECTS 12:

HURT NOT OTHERS IN WAYS THAT YOU YOURSELF WOULD FIND HURTFUL. UDANA-VARGA 5,1

THIS IS THE SUM OF DUTY; DO NAUGHT ONTO OTHERS WHAT YOU WOULD NOT HAVE THEM DO UNTO YOU. MAHABHARATA 5,1517

REGARD YOUR NEIGHBOR'S GAIN AS YOUR GAIN, AND YOUR NEIGHBOR'S LOSS AS YOUR OWN LOSS. TAI SHANG KAN YIN P'IEN

NO ONE OF YOU IS A BELIEVER UNTIL HE DESIRES FOR HIS BROTHER THAT WHICH HE DESIRES FOR HIMSELF. SUNNAH

THAT NATURE ALONE IS GOOD WHICH REFRAINS FROM DOING ANOTHER WHATSOEVER IS NOT GOOD FOR ITSELF. DADISTEN-I-DINIK, 94,5

WHAT IS HATEFUL TO YOU, DO NOT DO TO YOUR FELLOWMAN. THIS IS THE ENTIRE LAW; ALL THE REST IS COMMENTARY. TALMUD, SHABBAT 31D

A TRUTH IS NOT PRAISEWORTHY BECAUSE OF THE TEACHER WHO SPOKE IT. RATHER, TEACHERS ARE PRAISEWORTHY TO THE EXTENT THAT THEIR WORDS **RESONATE** WITH WHAT WE, IN OUR HEARTS, KNOW TO BE TRUE.

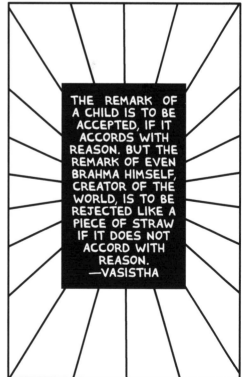

THE REMARK OF A CHILD IS TO BE ACCEPTED, IF IT ACCORDS WITH REASON. BUT THE REMARK OF EVEN BRAHMA HIMSELF, CREATOR OF THE WORLD, IS TO BE REJECTED LIKE A PIECE OF STRAW IF IT DOES NOT ACCORD WITH REASON. —VASISTHA

# TRUST YOURSELF

**1**

ALL THAT YOU NEED FOR GROWTH AND GUIDANCE IN LIFE IS ALREADY PRESENT INSIDE YOU.

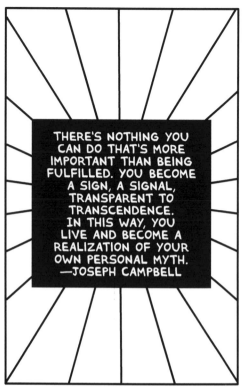

THERE'S NOTHING YOU CAN DO THAT'S MORE IMPORTANT THAN BEING FULFILLED. YOU BECOME A SIGN, A SIGNAL, TRANSPARENT TO TRANSCENDENCE. IN THIS WAY, YOU LIVE AND BECOME A REALIZATION OF YOUR OWN PERSONAL MYTH.
—JOSEPH CAMPBELL

AS YOU MATURE, YOU GROW TO FILL A PARTICULAR NICHE IN THE WORLD. THIS PROCESS IS GUIDED BY THE SOUL, AS IT EXPRESSES ITSELF THROUGH YOUR NATURE, CHARACTER, AND TALENTS. IT CANNOT BE FORCED; IT WORKS ONLY WHEN YOU'RE FREE TO PURSUE YOUR OWN **INTERESTS** AND **ABILITIES**.

THE PURPOSE OF EDUCATION IS TO REMOVE ALL OBSTACLES IN THE UNFOLDING OF EACH CHILD'S INNATE GENIUS. EDUCATION IS THE **DRAWING OUT** OF THE SOUL.

ALAS, THIS IS SELDOM THE CASE IN PRACTICE. WHEN YOUNG PEOPLE ARE **FORCED** INTO EXISTING OCCUPATIONS AND INSTITUTIONS, INSTEAD OF BEING **SET FREE** TO CREATE A WORLD OF THEIR OWN, THE RESULT IS A TREMENDOUS LOSS OF ENERGY AND INTEGRITY.

I WOULD NOT HAVE ANYONE ADOPT MY MODE OF LIVING FOR MY SAKE. I WOULD HAVE EACH PERSON BE CAREFUL TO FIND OUT AND PURSUE HIS OR HER **OWN** WAY.

**HENRY DAVID THOREAU**

THERE COMES A POINT WHEN YOU MUST TAKE YOURSELF FOR YOUR PORTION, FOR BETTER OR WORSE, RICHER OR POORER. IT DOESN'T DO ANY GOOD TO ENVY OTHERS WHO SEEM SMARTER, BETTER, OR MORE TALENTED. FOCUS ON CULTIVATING YOUR OWN **GARDEN**. IT MAY SEEM A PITIFUL LITTLE PLOT, BUT WITH LOVE AND LABOR IT WILL PRODUCE A BOUNTIFUL HARVEST.

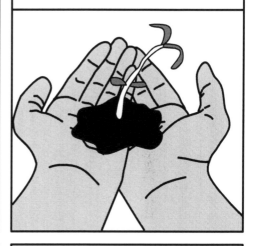

DISCOVER WHAT YOU'RE GOOD AT AND LOVE DOING. DO NOTHING THAT YOU CANNOT DO **WHOLEHEARTEDLY**. FIND A VOCATION THAT YOU CAN TRULY PUT YOUR HEART AND SOUL INTO.

ARCHITECTURE ENGINEERING ARTS, DESIGN, ENTERTAINMENT, SPORTS, MEDIA BUILDING GROUNDS CLEANING MAINTENANCE BUSINESS FINANCIAL OPERATIONS COMMUNITY SOCIAL SERVICES COMPUTER MATHEMATICAL CONSTRUCTION EXTRACTION EDUCATION, TRAINING, LIBRARY FARMING, FISHING, FORESTRY FOOD PREPARATION SERVING RELATED HEALTHCARE PRACTITIONERS TECHNICAL HEALTHCARE SUPPORT INSTALLATION, MAINTENANCE, REPAIR LEGAL LIFE, PHYSICAL, SOCIAL SCIENCE MANAGEMENT MILITARY SPECIFIC OFFICE ADMINISTRATIVE SUPPORT PERSONAL CARE SERVICE PRODUCTION PROTECTIVE SERVICE SALES RELATED ARCHITECTURAL DRAFTERS AUTOMOTIVE ENGINEERING TECHNICIANS AUTOMOTIVE ENGINEERS BIOCHEMICAL ENGINEERS BIOMEDICAL ENGINEERS CARTOGRAPHERS PHOTOGRAMMETRISTS CHEMICAL ENGINEERS CIVIL DRAFTERS CIVIL ENGINEERING TECHNICIANS CIVIL ENGINEERS COMPUTER HARDWARE ENGINEERS DRAFTERS, ALL ELECTRICAL ELECTRONIC ENGINEERING TECHNICIANS ELECTRICAL ELECTRONICS DRAFTERS ELECTRICAL DRAFTERS ELECTRICAL ENGINEERING TECHNICIANS ELECTRICAL ENGINEERING TECHNOLOGISTS ELECTRICAL ENGINEERS ELECTRO-MECHANICAL TECHNICIANS ELECTROMECHANICAL ENGINEERING TECHNOLOGISTS ELECTRONIC DRAFTERS ELECTRONICS ENGINEERING TECHNICIANS ELECTRONICS ENGINEERING TECHNOLOGISTS ELECTRONICS ENGINEERS, EXCEPT COMPUTER ENERGY ENGINEERS ENGINEERING TECHNICIANS, EXCEPT DRAFTERS, ALL ENGINEERS, ALL ENVIRONMENTALENGINEERING TECHNICIANS ENVIRONMENTAL ENGINEERS FIRE-PREVENTION PROTECTION ENGINEERS FUEL CELL ENGINEERS FUEL CELL TECHNICIANS GEODETIC SURVEYORS HEALTH SAFETY ENGINEERS, EXCEPT MINING SAFETY ENGINEERS INSPECTORS HUMAN FACTORS ENGINEERS ERGONOMISTS INDUSTRIAL ENGINEERING TECHNICIANS INDUSTRIAL ENGINEERING TECHNOLOGISTS INDUSTRIAL ENGINEERS INDUSTRIAL SAFETY HEALTH ENGINEERS LANDSCAPE ARCHITECTS MANUFACTURING ENGINEERING TECHNOLOGISTS MANUFACTURING ENGINEERS MANUFACTURING PRODUCTION TECHNICIANS MAPPING TECHNICIANS MARINE

MANY PEOPLE THINK OF WORK AS AN OBSTACLE TO THE SPIRITUAL LIFE—AS IF SPIRITUALITY WERE SOMETHING SEPARATE FROM OUR DAILY ACTIVITIES. BUT IF YOU **LISTEN** TO YOUR SOUL'S VOICE AND **FOLLOW** ITS CALLING, WORK BECOMES AN OPPORTUNITY TO SHARPEN YOUR SKILLS, STRENGTHEN YOUR CHARACTER, AND GAIN WISDOM.

YOU MUST ENTER THE FOREST ADVENTUROUS AT ITS DARKEST POINT, WHERE THERE IS NO PATH. WHERE THERE'S A PATH, IT IS SOMEONE ELSE'S PATH. EACH HUMAN BEING IS A UNIQUE PHENOMENON. THE IDEA IS TO FIND YOUR OWN PATHWAY TO BLISS. —JOSEPH CAMPBELL

THE SOUL EQUIPS US EACH WITH A **COMPASS** THAT POINTS TO OUR PROPER PATH. IN MATTERS OF MORALITY, WE CALL THIS "CONSCIENCE"; IN MATTERS OF INTELLECT, "GENIUS"; IN MATTERS OF VOCATION, "TALENT."

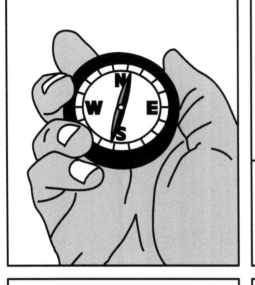

FOLLOW YOUR INNER CALLING, LISTEN TO THE WHISPER HEARD BY YOU ALONE, AND DO THE WORK YOU ARE INSPIRED TO DO. REMEMBER—NOTHING GREAT CAN BE ACCOMPLISHED WITHOUT **ENTHUSIASM**.

HAPPY IS THE ARTIST OR LABORER WHO FINDS **SATISFACTION** IN THE **WORK ITSELF**. ARE YOU SUCCESSFUL? LOOK TO YOUR WORK ALONE FOR THE ANSWER— NOT TO YOUR PRESS NOTICES OR BANK ACCOUNT.

IF YOU LOVE YOUR VOCATION AND SEEK TO IMPROVE YOUR CRAFT, EVENTUALLY YOUR WORK WILL BE RECOGNIZED. **AUTHENTICITY** IS THE KEY. POUR YOUR WHOLE SELF INTO YOUR WORK, AND YOUR WORK WILL SHINE.

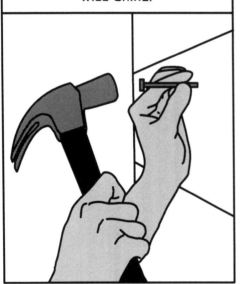

SELF-TRUST IS THE FIRST KEY TO SUCCESS. THE SECOND IS FOCUS— CONCENTRATION OF ENERGY. AND THE THIRD KEY IS A POSITIVE, FORWARD-LOOKING ATTITUDE.

**KEYS TO SUCCESS**

1. SELF-TRUST

2. FOCUS— CONCENTRATION OF ENERGY

3. A POSITIVE, FORWARD-LOOKING ATTITUDE

**POSITIVITY** IS CREATIVE; **NEGATIVITY** IS DESTRUCTIVE. INSTEAD OF SPENDING YOUR TIME AND ENERGY CURSING AND FIGHTING THE THINGS YOU DON'T LIKE, PRAISE AND PURSUE THE THINGS YOU DO.

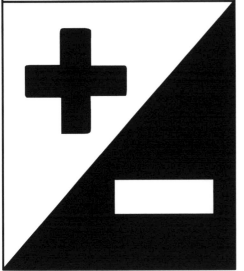

NATURE FAVORS **PROGRESS**. THINGS THAT TRY TO STAND STILL ARE SWEPT AWAY OR CRUSHED IN THE CURRENT. IF YOU WISH TO SUCCEED, RIDE THE **WAVE** OF EVOLUTION—DON'T RESIST IT.

A MIGHTY TREE GROWS FROM A TINY SEED. A PAGODA OF NINE STORIES IS BUILT FROM SMALL BRICKS. A JOURNEY OF THREE THOUSAND MILES BEGINS WITH ONE STEP.
—LAO TZU

YOU MIGHT BE THINKING, "SURE, SELF-TRUST IS FITTING FOR BRILLIANT, ORIGINAL MINDS—BUT MOST OF US ARE BETTER OFF FOLLOWING ORDERS AND PLAYING IT SAFE."

15

THE TRUTH IS, EACH OF US IS AN ORIGINAL MIND, WITH A **GENIUS** ALL OUR OWN. YOU ARE A UNIQUE EXPRESSION OF THE INFINITE, CREATIVE INTELLIGENCE OF THE UNIVERSE. IF YOU'RE UNAWARE OF THE POWERS WITHIN YOU, IT'S ONLY BECAUSE YOU HAVEN'T BEGUN TO EXERCISE THEM.

**MEDITATE** AND LISTEN CAREFULLY TO YOUR CONSCIENCE; WHEN YOU HAVE A CONVICTION ABOUT SOMETHING, **THINK**, **SPEAK**, AND **ACT** UPON IT; THEN YOU WILL BEGIN TO CUT YOUR OWN PATH IN THE WORLD.

SELF-TRUST DOESN'T MEAN INFLATING YOUR EGO, ACTING SELFISHLY, OR HARMING OTHERS. IT MEANS **TRUSTING** IN THE SOUL TO GUIDE YOUR WAY.

IF YOU ADVANCE CONFIDENTLY IN THE DIRECTION OF YOUR DREAMS, AND ENDEAVOR TO LIVE THE LIFE WHICH YOU IMAGINE, YOU WILL MEET WITH A SUCCESS UNEXPECTED IN COMMON HOURS.
—HENRY DAVID THOREAU

# AS YOU SOW, YOU WILL REAP

2

YOUR THOUGHTS AND ACTIONS SHAPE YOUR CHARACTER, AND YOUR CHARACTER DETERMINES YOUR DESTINY.

WE ARE NOT PUNISHED FOR OUR SINS, BUT BY THEM.

—ELBERT HUBBARD

IT'S COMMONLY SUPPOSED THAT THERE IS NO **JUSTICE** IN THIS WORLD. THE WICKED APPEAR TO PROSPER, WHILE THE GOOD SUFFER. IF JUSTICE IS EVER TO BE ATTAINED, IT WILL BE IN THE NEXT LIFE.

FROM THE SOUL'S PERSPECTIVE, HOWEVER, THERE IS A PERFECT JUSTICE AT WORK THROUGHOUT THE UNIVERSE. **SILENTLY BUT SURELY**, EVERY CRIME IS PUNISHED AND EVERY VIRTUE IS REWARDED.

EVERY ACTION HAS A TWOFOLD REACTION: INTERNAL AND EXTERNAL. THE **INTERNAL REACTION**—THE EFFECT UPON A PERSON'S CHARACTER—HAPPENS **IMMEDIATELY**. THE **EXTERNAL REACTION**—THE EFFECT THAT'S VISIBLE TO THE OUTSIDE WORLD—HAPPENS **EVENTUALLY**. IT MAY TAKE YEARS FOR AN EXTERNAL REACTION TO TAKE EFFECT, BUT THE **LAW OF CAUSE AND EFFECT** IS NEVER BROKEN.

THE TRUE REWARDS FOR VIRTUE AND PUNISHMENTS FOR EVIL ARE **HIDDEN WITHIN** US. THE INTERNAL EFFECTS ARE PRIMARY; OUTWARD MANIFESTATIONS—RICHES OR RUIN, PRAISE OR BLAME—ARE SECONDARY.

WHEN YOU DO SOMETHING GOOD, YOU ARE THE ONE WHO **BENEFITS** MOST. WHEN YOU GIVE TO THE NEEDY, YOU ENRICH YOUR HEART WITH GENEROSITY. WHEN YOU REIGN IN YOUR APPETITES, YOU GROW IN SELF-CONTROL.

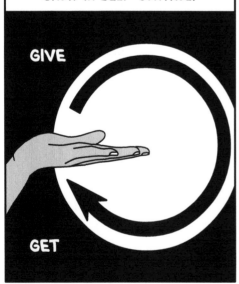

WHEN YOU **FORGIVE** SOMEONE WHO WRONGED YOU, DOES YOUR FORGIVENESS CLEANSE **THEIR** HEART AND FREE **THEIR** MIND? NO—NOT DIRECTLY ANYWAY—IT INSTEAD CLEANSES **YOUR OWN** HEART OF BITTERNESS, AND FREES **YOUR OWN** MIND OF RESENTMENT.

THE OPPOSITE IS ALSO TRUE: WHEN YOU DO SOMETHING WRONG, YOU HARM YOURSELF. CHEAT SOMEONE, AND YOU CHEAT YOURSELF. SLANDER SOMEONE, AND YOU SULLY YOUR OWN REPUTATION. REFUSE TO HELP SOMEONE IN NEED, AND YOUR OWN HEART SHRINKS.

> THOSE WHO STEAL FROM OTHERS IMPOVERISH THEMSELVES; THOSE WHO GIVE TO OTHERS BECOME RICH.
>
> THOSE WHO FIGHT DO NOT WIN; THOSE WHO WIN DO NOT FIGHT. THIS IS THE WAY OF THE TAO.
>
> —LAO TZU

EVERY THOUGHT, WORD, AND DEED ACCRUES TO FORM YOUR CHARACTER. IN THE SOUL'S ECONOMY, **NOTHING IS LOST**. THE MOMENT YOU DO GOOD, IT'S REWARDED BY AN ELEVATION OF CHARACTER; AND THE MOMENT YOU DO WRONG, IT'S PUNISHED BY A DEGRADATION OF THE SAME.

AS YOU SOW, YOU WILL REAP— THIS IS THE **FOUNDATION** OF ALL MORALITY.

IT EXTENDS TO SOCIETY, TOO. AS YOU ARE, SO YOU ASSOCIATE. VIRTUOUS PEOPLE **ATTRACT** OTHER VIRTUOUS PEOPLE; THE WICKED ATTRACT THE WICKED. HERE IN THIS WORLD, AS THE RESULTS OF OUR CHOICES ACCUMULATE, WE ASCEND TO HEAVEN OR DESCEND INTO HELL.

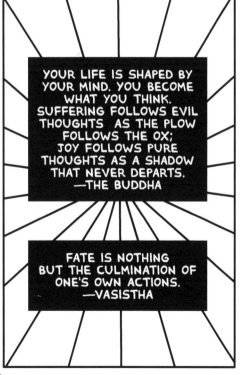

> YOUR LIFE IS SHAPED BY YOUR MIND. YOU BECOME WHAT YOU THINK. SUFFERING FOLLOWS EVIL THOUGHTS AS THE PLOW FOLLOWS THE OX; JOY FOLLOWS PURE THOUGHTS AS A SHADOW THAT NEVER DEPARTS.
> —THE BUDDHA

> FATE IS NOTHING BUT THE CULMINATION OF ONE'S OWN ACTIONS.
> —VASISTHA

# NOTHING OUTSIDE YOU CAN HARM YOU

3

CIRCUMSTANCES AND EVENTS DON'T MATTER AS MUCH AS WHAT YOU DO WITH THEM.

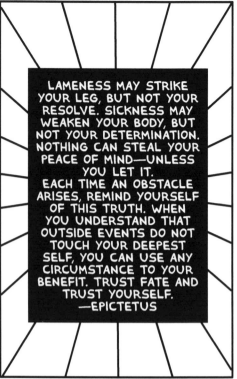

LAMENESS MAY STRIKE YOUR LEG, BUT NOT YOUR RESOLVE. SICKNESS MAY WEAKEN YOUR BODY, BUT NOT YOUR DETERMINATION. NOTHING CAN STEAL YOUR PEACE OF MIND—UNLESS YOU LET IT.

EACH TIME AN OBSTACLE ARISES, REMIND YOURSELF OF THIS TRUTH. WHEN YOU UNDERSTAND THAT OUTSIDE EVENTS DO NOT TOUCH YOUR DEEPEST SELF, YOU CAN USE ANY CIRCUMSTANCE TO YOUR BENEFIT. TRUST FATE AND TRUST YOURSELF.
—EPICTETUS

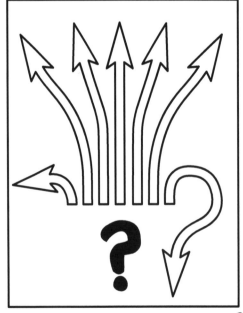

NEVER UNDERESTIMATE THE POWER OF YOUR **FREE WILL**. YOU LIVE IN A WORLD OF YOUR OWN CREATION, WHICH YOU BUILD DAY BY DAY.

THOUGHTS INSPIRE ACTIONS; ACTIONS FORM HABITS; HABITS SHAPE YOUR LIFE. A CHEERFUL OR CANTANKEROUS **ATTITUDE** EXPRESSES ITSELF IN A SMILE OR FROWN; HELD LONG ENOUGH, IT WILL BECOME **ETCHED** ON YOUR FACE.

WHEN IT COMES TO CHARACTER, ALL IS CAUSE AND EFFECT. LUCK AND CIRCUMSTANCE HAVE NOTHING TO DO WITH IT. IF YOU CHANGE YOUR DOMINANT THOUGHT PATTERNS, CHANGES IN YOUR OUTWARD LIFE WILL SOON FOLLOW. YOU'LL **ATTRACT** NEW SITUATIONS, SURROUNDINGS, FRIENDS, AND OPPORTUNITIES THAT RESONATE WITH YOUR MENTALITY.

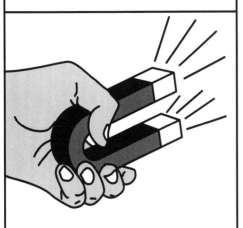

CIRCUMSTANCES ARE NEUTRAL. IT'S HOW YOU **RESPOND** TO THEM THAT DETERMINES WHETHER THEY DO YOU GOOD OR ILL. WE'VE ALL SEEN EXAMPLES OF PEOPLE LIVING IN THE HARSHEST OF CIRCUMSTANCES—POVERTY, WAR, DISEASE—YET WHOSE SOULS SHINE FORTH WITH POWER AND GRACE.

TAKE **RESPONSIBILITY** FOR YOUR LIFE, AND YOU'LL GAIN THE POWER TO CHANGE IT. BE PATIENT AND CONTENT IN ALL CIRCUMSTANCES, AND YOU'LL FIND UNSHAKABLE **PEACE**.

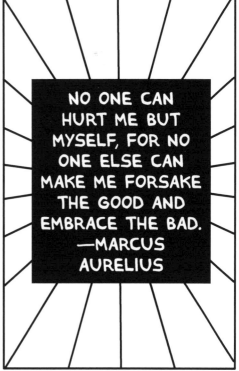

NO ONE CAN HURT ME BUT MYSELF, FOR NO ONE ELSE CAN MAKE ME FORSAKE THE GOOD AND EMBRACE THE BAD. —MARCUS AURELIUS

IF NOTHING OUTSIDE US CAN HARM US, HOW IS IT THAT WE'RE ALL VULNERABLE TO **DISEASE, DISASTER, AND DEATH**? NO AMOUNT OF VIRTUE CAN SAVE US FROM THESE EVENTS.

THE ANSWER IS THAT THESE THINGS ONLY AFFECT THE EXTERNAL, IMPERMANENT, EVER-CHANGING ASPECTS OF OURSELVES. THEY DO NOT TOUCH THE **SOUL**.

IN FACT, AN APPARENT EVIL IS A BLESSING IN DISGUISE IF IT SPURS US ON TO LEARNING AND GROWTH. THOSE WHO REST ON THE CUSHION OF ADVANTAGE FALL **ASLEEP**; IT'S WHEN WE'RE PUSHED, CHALLENGED, OR EVEN DEFEATED, THAT WE'RE MOTIVATED TO IMPROVE.

LOSS OF HONESTY, LOSS OF GENEROSITY, LOSS OF SELF-CONTROL—THESE ARE THE **REAL DISASTERS** IN LIFE, WHICH DEGRADE YOUR CHARACTER AND DISCONNECT YOU FROM YOUR SOUL. AND ONLY YOU CAN BRING THEM UPON YOURSELF.

THEY MAY KILL ME, BUT THEY CANNOT HURT ME. —SOCRATES

# THE UNIVERSE IS INSIDE YOU

4

THE WORLD AROUND YOU IS A REFLECTION OF THE WORLD WITHIN YOU.

FIND TONGUES IN TREES, BOOKS IN RUNNING BROOKS, SERMONS IN STONES, AND GOOD IN EVERY THING.

WILLIAM SHAKESPEARE

NATURE IS THE **MIRROR** OF THE SOUL. THERE'S A DIRECT CORRESPONDENCE BETWEEN OUR INTERIOR AND EXTERIOR WORLDS, BETWEEN THE SOUL AND ALL THAT OUR EYES CAN SEE.

THIS IS DEMONSTRATED IN **LANGUAGE**, WHERE SPIRITUAL CONCEPTS ARE REPRESENTED BY NATURAL FACTS.

KNOWLEDGE IS **LIGHT**, IGNORANCE IS **DARKNESS**, ROMANTIC LOVE IS A **FLOWER**, INSPIRATION IS A **SPARK**. A NOBLE PERSON IS A **LION**; A SLY ONE A **FOX**; AN INNOCENT ONE A **SHEEP**; A FOOLISH ONE AN **ASS**; A RESOLUTE ONE A **ROCK**.

HEART, BRAIN, AND GUT REFER TO OUR **EMOTIONS**, **THOUGHTS**, AND **INSTINCTS**, RESPECTIVELY.

THESE METAPHORS AREN'T THE FANCIES OF A FEW POETS—THEY'RE CONSISTENT ACROSS CULTURES. AS WE TRACE HUMAN LANGUAGE BACK TO ITS ORIGINS, IT BECOMES MORE AND MORE **PICTORIAL**, UNTIL AT LAST IT'S ALL PICTURES.

THE PROVERBS OF ALL NATIONS USE IMAGES FROM NATURE TO MAKE TRUTHS **TANGIBLE**. "THE EARLY BIRD GETS THE WORM"; "A ROLLING STONE GATHERS NO MOSS"; "MAKE HAY WHILE THE SUN SHINES"; "BIRDS OF A FEATHER FLOCK TOGETHER"; "THE STRAW THAT BROKE THE CAMEL'S BACK"; AND SO ON.

LIKEWISE, THE AXIOMS OF PHYSICS CORRESPOND TO SPIRITUAL TRUTHS. "EVERY ACTION CAUSES AN EQUAL AND OPPOSITE REACTION"; "THE WHOLE IS GREATER THAN THE SUM OF ITS PARTS"; "AN OBJECT AT REST WILL STAY AT REST UNTIL A FORCE ACTS UPON IT"; "THE SMALLEST WEIGHT CAN LIFT THE HEAVIEST USING LEVERAGE." THESE PROPOSITIONS APPLY TO OUR **LIVES** AS MUCH AS THEY APPLY TO INANIMATE OBJECTS.

EVERYTHING IN NATURE CAN BE READ AS AN ALLEGORY FOR SOMETHING SPIRITUAL, MORAL, OR MENTAL. WHAT IS A FARM, BUT A **SILENT SCRIPTURE**? THE WHEAT AND THE CHAFF, THE SUN AND THE RAIN, THE BEES AND THE LOCUSTS, SPRINGTIME AND HARVEST—ALL ARE SACRED SYMBOLS. "AS YOU SOW, YOU SHALL REAP," THE FIELDS PROCLAIM.

BY EXPLORING THE WORLD AROUND US, WE LEARN WHO WE ARE. EACH NEW EXPERIENCE WE HAVE, AND EACH NEW FACT WE LEARN, BROADENS OUR MENTAL AND SPIRITUAL HORIZONS. THE MORE WE **STUDY NATURE**, THE BETTER WE KNOW OURSELVES.

SCIENTIFIC DISCOVERIES SHINE NEW LIGHT ON THE INFINITE LAW OF THE UNIVERSE, WHICH BROUGHT ALL THINGS INTO BEING AND LIVES IN US. ANY RELIGION THAT IS AFRAID OF SCIENCE FORFEITS ITS MISSION TO PURSUE TRUTH AND, IN SO DOING, DISHONORS GOD.

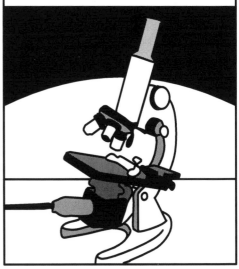

THE LAWS OF TIME AND SPACE ARE IN US—WE CARRY THOSE LAWS WITHIN OUR OWN HEADS—AND ANYTHING WE CAN SEE OR KNOW ANYWHERE WILL INVOLVE THOSE LAWS. WE ARE THE EYES AND THE CONSCIOUSNESS AND THE EARS AND THE BREATHING OF LIFE ITSELF. WE'RE EARTH'S CHILDREN, AND, SINCE THE EARTH ITSELF CAME OUT OF SPACE, IS IT ANY WONDER THAT THE LAWS OF SPACE LIVE IN US? THERE'S A WONDERFUL ACCORD BETWEEN THE INTERIOR AND EXTERIOR WORLDS.
—JOSEPH CAMPBELL

THE PHYSICAL WORLD IS A REALM OF **DUALITY:** NORTH AND SOUTH, HOT AND COLD, DARK AND LIGHT, STRENGTH AND WEAKNESS, GOOD AND EVIL, TRUTH AND FALSEHOOD, UGLINESS AND BEAUTY. EACH QUALITY DEPENDS ON ITS OPPOSITE; WITHOUT ONE, YOU COULDN'T POSSIBLY KNOW THE OTHER.

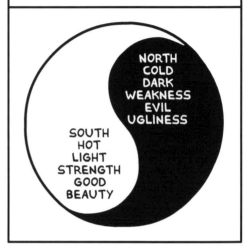

NORTH
COLD
DARK
WEAKNESS
EVIL
UGLINESS

SOUTH
HOT
LIGHT
STRENGTH
GOOD
BEAUTY

BUT **UNDERNEATH** THE SEAS OF OUR LIVES, WHICH ALTERNATE BETWEEN STORM AND CALM, EBB AND FLOW, LIES THE UNFATHOMABLE ABYSS OF **PURE BEING**. THIS IS THE SOUL. IT HAS NO LIMITS OR COUNTER-BALANCES. IT TRANSCENDS ALL CATEGORIES, SWALLOWS ALL OPPOSITES. IT SIMPLY IS.

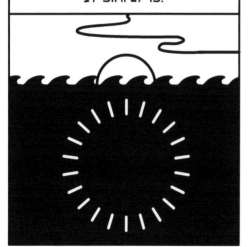

ALL OF NATURE EMERGES FROM THIS ONE SOURCE. IN THE PHYSICAL WORLD, WITH ITS COUNTLESS SEPARATE BEINGS, INEQUALITIES ARE INEVITABLE. WHEN IT COMES TO ANYTHING YOU CAN MEASURE, SOME INDIVIDUALS WILL HAVE **MORE** AND OTHERS HAVE **LESS**.

MORE
LESS

BUT SEEN FROM THE SOUL'S PERSPECTIVE, INEQUALITIES MELT IN AN OCEAN OF **UNCONDITIONAL LOVE**. THE DISTINCTION BETWEEN YOURS AND MINE VANISHES. WE ARE ALL ONE.

THIS WAS THE PERSPECTIVE OF **JESUS** WHEN HE SAID:

I AM IN THE FATHER, AND THE FATHER IS IN ME. YOU ARE IN ME, AND I AM IN YOU.

COSMIC CONSCIOUSNESS ALONE EXISTS NOW AND EVER. THAT CONSCIOUSNESS REFLECTED IN ITSELF APPEARS TO BE CREATION.
—VASISTHA

DOES THE VASTNESS OF THE UNIVERSE MAKE YOU FEEL INSIGNIFICANT? THE MICROSCOPE HAS YET TO FIND A PART OF NATURE THAT'S UNMIRACULOUS BY VIRTUE OF BEING TOO SMALL.

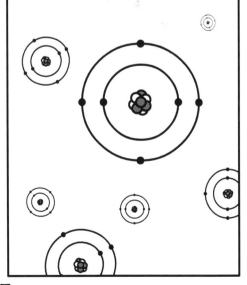

THE WHOLE UNIVERSE IS REPRESENTED IN EACH OF ITS **PARTS**. EVERYTHING IN NATURE CONTAINS ALL THE POWERS OF NATURE—INCLUDING YOU.

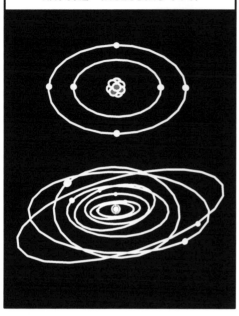

YOU BELONG TO A **FAMILY** THAT INCLUDES EVERY PLANT AND ANIMAL ON EARTH. ALL EVOLVED FROM THE FIRST LIVING CELL; ALL FOLLOW THE SAME LAWS OF ORGANIZATION AND DEVELOPMENT; AND ALL ARE ANIMATED BY THE SAME LIFE FORCE.

THE SAME POWER THAT BROUGHT THE UNIVERSE INTO BEING IS MANIFEST IN EVERY PARTICLE. THIS IS THE TRUE MEANING OF DIVINE **OMNIPRESENCE**—GOD IS EVERYWHERE.

THERE IS BEING THAT ENCOMPASSES ALL, AND IT EXISTED BEFORE EARTH OR THE UNIVERSE. CALM, INDEED, AND IMMATERIAL; IT IS SINGULAR AND CHANGELESS.

ALL CREATION FLOWS FROM IT AND RETURNS TO IT. IT IS THE WORLD'S MOTHER. I CANNOT DEFINE IT, BUT I WILL CALL IT TAO.

HUMANITY IS THE CHILD OF THE EARTH; THE EARTH IS THE CHILD OF THE UNIVERSE; THE UNIVERSE IS THE CHILD OF THE TAO.

THE TAO HAS NO MOTHER, BUT IS MOTHER OF ALL.

—LAO TZU

# IDENTIFY WITH THE INFINITE

5

CENTER YOUR IDENTITY ON THE SOUL AND YOUR LIFE'S PURPOSE WILL UNFOLD.

WHEN ONE IS CONVINCED THAT THE INFINITE SELF ALONE IS REAL, ONE GOES BEYOND SORROW. —VASISTHA

WHO ARE YOU?

WHEN ASKED THIS QUESTION, YOU'RE LIKELY TO REPLY WITH A CONGLOMERATION OF THINGS, SUCH AS YOUR NAME, AGE, FAMILY, NATIONALITY, RELIGION, PERSONALITY TYPE, OCCUPATION, INCOME, ACCOMPLISHMENTS, HOBBIES, LIKES AND DISLIKES, AND SO ON.

THESE ARE ALL THINGS THAT YOU HAVE. BUT WHO HAS THESE THINGS? WHO ARE YOU, **REALLY**?

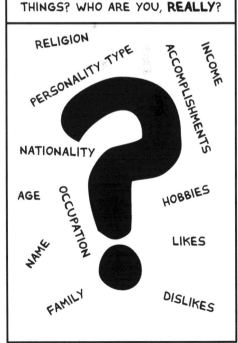

RELIGION
PERSONALITY TYPE
ACCOMPLISHMENTS
INCOME
NATIONALITY
AGE
OCCUPATION
HOBBIES
LIKES
NAME
FAMILY
DISLIKES

THERE ARE TWO SENSES OF THE WORD "SELF." ONE IS **LIMITED**, THE OTHER **INFINITE**. IF YOU IDENTIFY YOURSELF AS A PHYSICAL BEING WITH CERTAIN ATTRIBUTES AND ATTAINMENTS, YOU ARE IDENTIFYING WITH YOUR LIMITED, FRAGMENTARY SELF. BUT IF YOU IDENTIFY YOURSELF AS A SPIRITUAL BEING—AS SOUL INCARNATE IN A PHYSICAL BODY— YOU ARE IDENTIFYING WITH YOUR INFINITE, **WHOLE** SELF.

MOST PEOPLE THINK TOO **LITTLE** OF THEMSELVES. THIS MIGHT COME AS A SURPRISE, BECAUSE IT'S COMMONLY SAID OF MATERIALLY-MINDED PEOPLE THAT THEY "THINK TOO MUCH OF THEMSELVES." BUT THE TRUTH IS THE OPPOSITE: THEY THINK OF THEIR BODIES, CLOTHES, MONEY, POSSESSIONS, STATUS— EVERYTHING **BUT** THEMSELVES.

IT'S NOT POSSIBLE TO THINK TOO **HIGHLY** OF YOUR INFINITE SELF. IF YOU IDENTIFY PRIMARILY WITH YOUR LIMITED SELF, YOUR HAPPINESS WILL BE AT THE MERCY OF YOUR PHYSICAL, MENTAL, AND MATERIAL CIRCUMSTANCES, WHICH ARE ALWAYS IN FLUX.

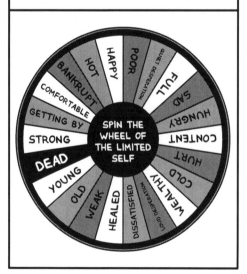

BUT YOU ARE NOT YOUR BODY. YOU ARE NOT YOUR MIND. YOU ARE A **SOUL** WHO **HAS** A BODY AND A MIND. CENTER YOUR IDENTITY ON THIS INFINITE SELF, AND YOU'LL DISCOVER LASTING PEACE AND JOY. WHEN YOU OBSERVE THE STORMS OF LIFE FROM THE SOUL'S PERSPECTIVE, YOU'LL NO LONGER BE TOSSED ABOUT AND OVERWHELMED BY THEM.

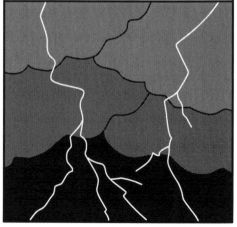

30

YOUR ATTRIBUTES AND ABILITIES ARE THINGS YOU HAVE; THEY DON'T DEFINE YOU. BUT WHEN YOU USE THEM AS MEANS OF **EXPRESSING** YOUR SOUL IN THIS WORLD, YOU'LL REACH YOUR FULL POTENTIAL.

THIS IS **LIVING FROM THE SOUL**.

THINK OF ELECTRIC LIGHTS IN A ROOM. WHAT IS IMPORTANT—IS IT THE ILLUMINATION, OR IS IT THE BULBS? THE BULBS ARE ONLY VEHICLES OF THE LIGHT. WITH WHAT DO YOU IDENTIFY YOURSELF, FINALLY? WITH THE BODY, OR WITH THE CONSCIOUSNESS? WHEN YOU HAVE IDENTIFIED YOURSELF WITH THE CONSCIOUSNESS, THE BODY IS SECONDARY. THAT WHICH WAS NOT BORN AND WILL NOT DIE CAME INTO MANIFESTATION THROUGH YOUR BODY, AND THIS SAME THING IS IN THE BODIES OF OTHERS.
—JOSEPH CAMPBELL

CULTIVATE YOUR CONNECTION TO SPIRIT. **MEDITATE** ON THE UNFATHOMABLE DEPTHS OF YOUR SOUL, AND ITS UNION WITH THE SOURCE.

YOUR SOUL IS PART OF THE **UNIVERSAL SOUL**, WHICH IS SERENE, WHOLE, AND PERFECT. IT IS AN ENDLESS OCEAN OF LIGHT, UPON WHICH OUR SOULS ARISE AS WAVES.

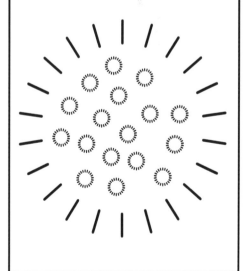

WE'RE ALL PART OF THIS UNIVERSAL SOUL, YET IT IS **FAR GREATER** THAN ANY HUMAN INCARNATION OR EXPRESSION. SHAKESPEARE'S PLAYS AND MICHELANGELO'S SCULPTURES—AS MAGNIFICENT AS THEY ARE—ONLY HINT AT THE BEAUTY AND WISDOM OF THE OCEANIC SOUL THAT INSPIRED THEM.

IF YOU FOCUS ON THE TASK AT HAND, SHED ALL DISTRACTIONS, AND FOLLOW REASON WITH STEADFAST DETERMINATION, THE DIVINE SPARK WITHIN YOU WILL BURST INTO FLAME. NURTURE THIS INNER LIGHT, KEEP IT PURE, AND BE READY TO RETURN IT TO ITS SOURCE WHEN YOUR TIME IS DONE. EXPECT NOTHING, FEAR NOTHING, SPEAK TRULY, AND ACT HEROICALLY. NO ONE CAN STOP YOU.
—MARCUS AURELIUS

WHAT IS THE PURPOSE OF YOUR LIFE? KEEP ON LIVING, AND YOUR LIFE WILL BE ITS OWN **ANSWER**. LIFE IS A STORY IN HIEROGLYPHS, ABLE TO BE UNDERSTOOD ONLY IN HINDSIGHT. ACTION COMES BEFORE UNDERSTANDING.

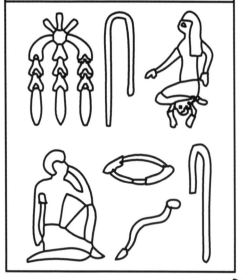

LIVING FROM THE SOUL MEANS THINKING, SPEAKING, AND ACTING IN ACCORDANCE WITH YOUR **TRUTH**.

TRUTH

WHEN YOU CONNECT WITH THE **SOUL** AND ALLOW IT TO SHINE THROUGH ALL THAT YOU SAY AND DO, YOU'LL BECOME FULLY AND TRULY YOURSELF.

WHEN YOU **SPEAK** FROM THE SOUL, YOUR VOICE WILL BE AS AUTHENTIC AS THE MURMUR OF THE BROOK AND THE RUSTLE OF THE CORN. AND WHEN YOU **ACT** FROM THE SOUL, YOUR BEHAVIOR WILL BE CONSISTENT WITH YOUR CONVICTIONS.

PUT YOUR BODY AND MIND IN SERVICE OF THE SOUL, AND YOU'LL LIVE YOUR **PURPOSE** IN THIS WORLD.

TO THOSE WHO IDENTIFY WITH THE BODY, THE BODY IS A SOURCE OF SUFFERING; BUT TO THE ENLIGHTENED, THE BODY IS REGARDED AS A VEHICLE OF WISDOM AND A SOURCE OF INFINITE DELIGHT.
—VASISTHA

# LIVE IN THE PRESENT

**6**

THE PRESENT MOMENT IS YOUR POINT OF POWER. ETERNITY IS NOW.

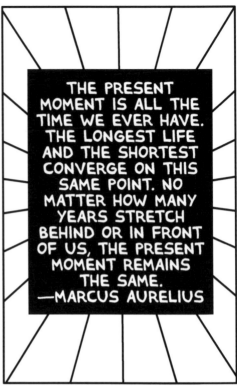

THE PRESENT MOMENT IS ALL THE TIME WE EVER HAVE. THE LONGEST LIFE AND THE SHORTEST CONVERGE ON THIS SAME POINT. NO MATTER HOW MANY YEARS STRETCH BEHIND OR IN FRONT OF US, THE PRESENT MOMENT REMAINS THE SAME.
—MARCUS AURELIUS

WHAT GOOD DOES IT DO YOU TO DWELL ON **YESTERDAY** OR WORRY ABOUT **TOMORROW**? IT ONLY UNSETTLES YOUR MIND, FRAYS YOUR NERVES, UPSETS YOUR STOMACH, AND DEPRESSES YOUR SPIRITS.

TO DISSOLVE WORRY, SHIFT YOUR ATTENTION TO THE **PRESENT**. THE PAST IS BUT A MEMORY; THE FUTURE IS BUT A DREAM. **NOW** IS THE ONLY TIME THAT YOU CAN THINK, FEEL, AND ACT. THE PRESENT MOMENT IS YOUR CONNECTION TO LIFE, YOUR POINT OF POWER.

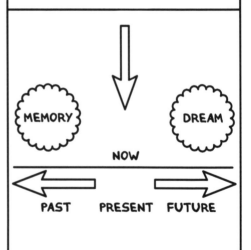

CONCENTRATE ON WHATEVER TASK IS BEFORE YOU. **HERE AND NOW** IS YOUR DUTY, YOUR EXCELLENCE, YOUR ONLY CONCERN.

IF YOUR BODY IS IN PAIN THIS MOMENT, OR YOUR MIND IS SUFFERING, REMEMBER THAT YOUR SOUL REMAINS AT **PEACE**. WHEN YOU IDENTIFY WITH THE SOUL, ALL FEAR DEPARTS.

OUCH! MY SHOULDER!

EVEN DEATH IS **NOTHING** TO THE SOUL. IF YOU REMAIN ENGAGED IN WORTHY THOUGHTS AND ACTIONS TO THE END, YOU WILL DIE LIKE A SOLDIER IN THE HEAT OF BATTLE WHO NEVER FEELS THE WOUND.

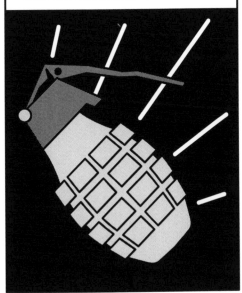

YOUR EARTHLY EXISTENCE IS TEMPORARY, BUT IF YOU LIVE FROM THE SOUL YOU'LL EXPERIENCE **ETERNITY** IN THE PRESENT MOMENT.

ETERNITY IS NOT FUTURE OR PAST. ETERNITY IS A DIMENSION OF NOW. IT IS A DIMENSION OF THE HUMAN SPIRIT—WHICH IS ETERNAL. FIND THAT ETERNAL DIMENSION WITHIN YOURSELF, AND YOU WILL RIDE THROUGH TIME AND THROUGHOUT THE WHOLE LENGTH OF YOUR DAYS.
—JOSEPH CAMPBELL

WHERE IS HEAVEN?
IS IT FAR BEYOND THE STARS?
NO, IT IS VERY NEAR.

IN RELIGIOUS LANGUAGE,
THINGS SAID TO BE "ABOVE" ARE
METAPHORS FOR WHAT IS
ACTUALLY **WITHIN** US.

WHEREVER THERE IS **LOVE**, THERE
IS HEAVEN. WHEREVER THERE IS
TRUTH, BEAUTY, JUSTICE, MERCY,
AND HOPE, THERE IS HEAVEN.

THE VIRTUES HAVE NOTHING TO
DO WITH TIME OR DEATH. THEY ARE
**IMMORTAL**. TO THE EXTENT THAT
YOU CULTIVATE THEM IN YOUR
HEART AND PUT THEM INTO ACTION,
YOU ARE IN HEAVEN. RIGHT HERE,
RIGHT NOW.

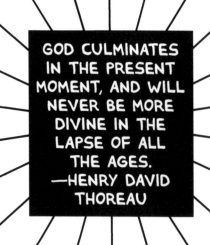

GOD CULMINATES
IN THE PRESENT
MOMENT, AND WILL
NEVER BE MORE
DIVINE IN THE
LAPSE OF ALL
THE AGES.
—HENRY DAVID
THOREAU

WHAT AWAITS US BEYOND THIS
LIFE IS A **MYSTERY**. BUT JUST AS
LIVING WELL TODAY IS THE BEST
PREPARATION FOR TOMORROW,
LIVING WELL IN THIS LIFE IS THE
BEST **PREPARATION** FOR ANY LIFE
TO COME.

FOLLOW THE PROMPTINGS OF YOUR SOUL AND FILL YOUR DAYS WITH **LOVE**, **LAUGHTER**, AND **MEANINGFUL LABOR**. THE REASON TO LIVE A GOOD AND VIRTUOUS LIFE IS NOT TO AVOID PUNISHMENT OR EARN A REWARD IN THE AFTERLIFE. LIVING WELL IS ITS OWN REASON. VIRTUE IS ITS OWN REWARD.

JUST FOLLOW MY LEAD!

SOMEDAY YOUR PHYSICAL BODY WILL DIE. YOUR FLAWS AND FAILINGS WILL PASS AWAY, TOO. BUT ALL THE LOVE, TRUTH, AND GOODNESS WITHIN YOU CAN **NEVER DIE**.

REAL YOU

RIP

THE FLEETING PHYSICAL YOU

EVERYTHING ABOUT YOU—YOUR BODY, MIND, ATTRIBUTES, POSSESSIONS—IS SUBJECT TO CHANGE AND DECAY, EXCEPT FOR THOSE THINGS THAT BELONG TO THE SOUL. SO GROUND YOUR IDENTITY IN YOUR CAPACITY FOR LOVE, TRUTH, AND GOODNESS. MAY YOUR SOUL **SHINE** BRIGHTER AND BRIGHTER, UNTIL THE MORTAL PORTION OF YOU IS PALTRY BY COMPARISON.

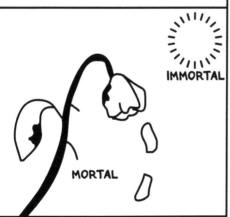

IMMORTAL

MORTAL

TO THE EXTENT THAT GOD LIVES WITHIN YOU, YOU ARE **IMMORTAL**.

THE THINGS MOST PEOPLE VALUE AND PURSUE IN THIS LIFE ARE PASSING AWAY. ALL THEIR STRIVING, ACQUIRING, AND FIGHTING—IT'S AS POINTLESS AS DOGS CHASING EACH OTHER. WHAT IS OF LASTING VALUE? GOODNESS, FAITHFULNESS, JUSTICE, AND TRUTH.
—MARCUS AURELIUS

# SEEK GOD WITHIN

7

THE HIGHEST REVELATION IS THE DIVINITY OF THE SOUL.

AT WHOSE BEHEST DOES THE MIND THINK? WHO BIDS THE BODY LIVE? WHO MAKES THE TONGUE SPEAK? WHO IS THAT EFFULGENT BEING THAT DIRECTS THE EYE TO FORM COLOR AND THE EAR TO SOUND? THE SELF IS THE EAR OF THE EAR, EYE OF THE EYE, MIND OF THE MIND, SPEECH OF SPEECH. GIVE UP THE FALSE IDENTIFICATION OF THE SELF WITH THE SENSES AND THE MIND, AND KNOW THE SELF TO BE DIVINE.
—THE UPANISHADS

THERE IS SOMETHING IN YOU THAT'S **HIGHER AND BETTER** THAN YOUR MORTAL SELF. THIS SOMETHING SPEAKS THE TRUTH WITH AUTHORITY. IT WILL NEVER LEAD YOU ASTRAY. NOTHING CAN HARM IT, NO MATTER HOW BADLY YOUR BODY MAY BE HURT. ITS PRINCIPLES ARE IN UNISON WITH THE LAWS OF NATURE. AND IT LIVES NOT JUST IN YOU, BUT IN EVERYONE.

THE SOUL IS THE PRESENCE OF GOD WITHIN YOU. IT IS THE **DIVINE PORTAL** OF WHICH JESUS SAID, "KNOCK AND THE DOOR WILL BE OPENED. SEEK AND YOU WILL FIND." IT IS THE DOORWAY TO HEAVEN, INVITING YOU TO EXPERIENCE ETERNITY HERE AND NOW.

WHAT WOULD IT PROFIT YOU TO GAIN THE WHOLE WORLD, BUT LOSE YOUR SOUL?
—JESUS

JESUS OF NAZARETH WAS ONE OF HUMANITY'S TRUE PROPHETS. DRAWN BY ITS BEAUTY, HE LOOKED UPON THE MYSTERY OF THE SOUL WITH OPEN EYES. HE LIVED IN **HARMONY WITH THE SOUL** AND GROUNDED HIS IDENTITY IN ITS DEPTHS.

WHEN JESUS SAID "THE KINGDOM OF GOD IS WITHIN YOU," HE WAS REFERRING TO THE SOUL. IN THE TWO THOUSAND YEARS SINCE HE WALKED THE EARTH, CHRISTIANITY HAS SPREAD ALL OVER THE GLOBE—YET THE HEART OF HIS MESSAGE, **THE DIVINITY OF THE SOUL**, GOES UNPREACHED.

CHRISTIANS WORSHIP JESUS AS THE ONLY INCARNATION OF GOD. BUT THE DIVINE SOUL, AS JESUS TAUGHT, IS WITHIN **ALL** AND FAVORS NO ONE.

BY ELEVATING THE PERSON OF JESUS ABOVE HIS MESSAGE, THE MESSAGE HAS BEEN LOST. AND BY DEPICTING CHRIST AS A KING WHO RULES BY THREATS OF HELLFIRE, CHRISTIANITY TURNED THE FRIEND OF HUMANITY INTO A **DESPOT**.

JESUS IS A MEDIATOR BETWEEN GOD AND HUMANITY SO FAR AS HE POINTS US TO TRUTH AND WE PUT IT INTO PRACTICE. "LOVE YOUR NEIGHBOR AS YOURSELF"; "LOVE YOUR ENEMIES"; "JUDGE NOT, LEST YOU BE JUDGED"; "FORGIVE, AND YOU WILL BE FORGIVEN"; "DO TO OTHERS AS YOU WOULD HAVE THEM DO TO YOU;" "DO NOT BE ANXIOUS ABOUT TOMORROW, FOR TOMORROW WILL TAKE CARE OF ITSELF."

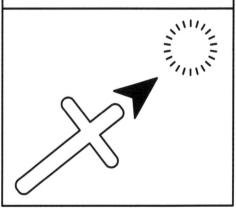

IF THE WORDS OF JESUS AND STORIES OF HIS LIFE AWAKEN YOU TO THE DIVINE SOUL WITHIN AND INSPIRE YOU TO TRANSFORM YOUR LIFE, HE WILL HAVE "SAVED" YOU BY HELPING YOU TO SAVE YOURSELF.

WHEN JESUS SAYS, "I AM THE ALL," HE MEANS, "I HAVE IDENTIFIED MYSELF WITH THE ALL." WHEN HE SAYS, IN THE GOSPEL OF THOMAS, "SPLIT THE STICK, YOU WILL FIND ME THERE; LIFT THE STONE, AND THERE I AM," THIS DOES NOT REFER TO HIS PHYSICAL BODY; IT REFERS INSTEAD TO THAT WHICH HE IS, AND YOU ARE. "THE KINGDOM OF HEAVEN IS WITHIN YOU." WHO IS IN HEAVEN? GOD. WHERE IS GOD? WITHIN YOU.
—JOSEPH CAMPBELL

THE SOUL DISCERNS WHAT IS **TRUE**, INDEPENDENT OF ANY TRADITION, INSTITUTION, OR BOOK. OUR RELIGIONS ARE STOREHOUSES OF SECONDHAND INSIGHTS, USEFUL FOR INSPIRATION BUT HARMFUL WHEN SUBSTITUTED FOR FIRSTHAND COMMUNION WITH THE DIVINE SOUL.

WHEN THE SOUL SPEAKS, OLD THINGS PASS AWAY. TEXTS AND TEMPLES **FALL**.

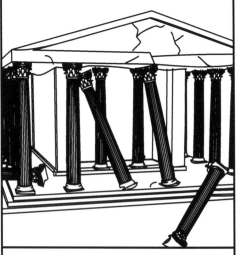

GOD SPEAKS TO US TODAY, IN OUR LANGUAGE, AS WELL AS GOD EVER SPOKE TO PEOPLE IN FARAWAY LANDS IN THE DISTANT PAST.

TO THE RELIGIOUSLY DEVOUT, THIS MAY SEEM LIKE A **DANGEROUS**, REVOLUTIONARY IDEA. BUT REALLY, THE TRUTH OF THE SOUL IS THE OLDEST OF REVELATIONS.

THE WORD UNTO THE PROPHET SPOKEN WAS WRIT ON TABLES YET UNBROKEN; THE WORD BY SEERS OR SIBYLS TOLD, IN GROVES OF OAK, OR FANES OF GOLD, STILL FLOATS UPON THE MORNING WIND, STILL WHISPERS TO THE WILLING MIND.

—FROM EMERSON'S POEM, "THE PROBLEM"

GOD IS FOUND **WITHIN**, NOT WITHOUT. THAT'S THE MESSAGE OF JESUS AND ALL MYSTICS THROUGH THE AGES. AS LONG AS YOU KEEP SEARCHING FOR GOD OUTSIDE YOURSELF, YOU'LL NEVER BE AT **PEACE**. BUT WHEN YOU LOOK WITHIN AND FIND THAT GOD IS IN YOU—AND YOU ARE IN GOD—YOU WILL KNOW THE PEACE THAT PASSES UNDERSTANDING.

THINK AND FEEL FOR YOURSELF. LOVE AND HELP OTHERS. MAKE YOUR LIFE A CLEAR VESSEL OF THE DIVINE SOUL WITHIN, EVEN IF UP TILL NOW YOU HAVE ONLY GLIMPSED IT ENOUGH TO KNOW THAT IT EXISTS. THE UNIVERSAL SOUL ENCOMPASSES ALL TRUTHS AND KNOWS ALL THINGS. IT'S POWER IS BOUNDLESS, BECAUSE ITS **LOVE** IS **BOUNDLESS**.

# EMERSON'S LIFE & INFLUENCE

I WAS BORN ON **MAY 25, 1803**, THE SECOND SON OF A BELOVED AND RESPECTED CHRISTIAN MINISTER IN BOSTON. MY FATHER DIED OF STOMACH CANCER WHEN I WAS ONLY SEVEN, LEAVING MY FOUR BROTHERS AND I TO BE RAISED BY OUR MOTHER AND AUNT.

AT AGE FOURTEEN, I LEFT HOME FOR **HARVARD** COLLEGE, GRADUATING FOUR YEARS LATER IN 1821. AFTER WORKING AS A TUTOR FOR THREE YEARS, I ENROLLED AT HARVARD DIVINITY SCHOOL WITH THE GOAL OF BECOMING A PASTOR LIKE MY FATHER AND MY GRANDFATHER.

IN 1829, AT AGE TWENTY-FIVE, I WAS ORDAINED A MINISTER AT BOSTON'S SECOND CHURCH. THAT SAME YEAR, I MARRIED **ELLEN TUCKER**. JUST EIGHTEEN MONTHS LATER, ELLEN DIED OF TUBERCULOSIS.

AROUND THE SAME TIME, I LOST MY FAITH IN TRADITIONAL CHRISTIANITY. UNABLE TO REPEAT THE CREEDS AND RITUALS OF THE PAST, I RESIGNED MY PASTORATE TO PURSUE A **FIRSTHAND** RELATIONSHIP WITH GOD.

AFTER LOSING MY WIFE AND LEAVING THE MINISTRY, I **SAILED** TO EUROPE FOR TEN MONTHS. I RETURNED WITH A NEW SENSE OF VOCATION: I WOULD BE A WRITER AND LECTURER, TEACHING RELIANCE ON THE **LIGHT WITHIN**.

TODAY PEOPLE REMEMBER ME MAINLY FOR MY ESSAYS, BUT DURING MY LIFETIME I WAS RENOWNED AS A **PUBLIC SPEAKER**. FROM 1833 TO 1877, I DELIVERED OVER 1,500 LECTURES. I TRAVELLED ALL OVER NEW ENGLAND AND THE MIDWEST, EVEN VENTURING ONCE TO CALIFORNIA. I DID NOT TOUR THE SOUTHERN SLAVE-OWNING STATES.

A SUPPORTER OF CIVIL RIGHTS AND WOMEN'S RIGHTS, I WAS A FRIEND OF MANY ABOLITIONISTS AND EARLY FEMINISTS, INCLUDING MARGARET FULLER, WHOM I HIRED TO EDIT MY TRANSCENDENTALIST JOURNAL, **THE DIAL**. I SIGNED THE "DECLARATION OF SENTIMENTS" OF THE FIRST WOMEN'S RIGHTS CONVENTION HELD AT **SENECA FALLS** IN 1848, AND I SPOKE AT THE 1855 CONVENTION IN BOSTON.

NEW YORK

FIRST CONVENTION FOR **WOMAN'S RIGHTS** WAS HELD ON THIS CORNER 1848

STATE EDUCATION DEPARTMENT 1932

WHILE LECTURING AT THE SMITHSONIAN INSTITUTION IN 1862, I MET WITH PRESIDENT **ABRAHAM LINCOLN** AND ENCOURAGED HIM TO PUSH FOR AN IMMEDIATE END TO SLAVERY. THE EMANCIPATION PROCLAMATION WAS ISSUED THE NEXT YEAR.

AMONG THOSE DIRECTLY INSPIRED BY ME WERE THE TWO GREATEST AMERICAN POETS OF THE NINETEENTH CENTURY, **WALT WHITMAN** AND **EMILY DICKINSON**.

AT AGE TWENTY-THREE, **WHITMAN** ATTENDED MY 1842 LECTURE ON "THE POET" IN NEW YORK CITY. WHITMAN'S **LEAVES OF GRASS** (FIRST EDITION, 1855) WAS WRITTEN IN ANSWER TO MY CALL FOR A NEW, DISTINCTLY AMERICAN POETRY.

MY IDEAS WERE SIMMERING AND EMERSON BROUGHT THEM TO A BOIL.

EMILY DICKINSON WAS GIVEN A COPY OF MY POEMS IN 1850, WHEN SHE WAS TWENTY. WHILE LECTURING AT AMHERST IN 1857, I STAYED IN THE HOME OF DICKINSON'S BROTHER AND SISTER-IN-LAW. EMILY LIVED NEXT DOOR, AND WE MAY HAVE MET, THOUGH NEITHER OF US LEFT A RECORD OF IT.

RALPH WALDO EMERSON HAS TOUCHED THE SECRET SPRING.

I ALSO INFLUENCED THE FOUNDING FIGURES OF THE NATURE CONSERVATION MOVEMENT, **HENRY DAVID THOREAU** AND **JOHN MUIR**. THOREAU FIRST MET ME AT HARVARD IN 1837, AND WE BECAME CLOSE COMPANIONS. IN 1845, THOREAU MOVED TO A SMALL CABIN ON MY PROPERTY AT **WALDEN POND**, WHICH LED TO THE WRITING OF HIS MASTERPIECE, **WALDEN**.

JOHN MUIR—THE WILDERNESS ADVOCATE AND FOUNDER OF THE SIERRA CLUB—READ MY WORKS AND WAS INSPIRED BY THEM. DURING MY CALIFORNIA SOJOURN OF 1871, WE SPENT SEVERAL DAYS TOGETHER IN YOSEMITE.

EMERSON WAS THE MOST SERENE, MAJESTIC, SEQUOIA-LIKE SOUL I EVER MET. HIS SMILE WAS AS SWEET AND CALM AS MORNING LIGHT ON MOUNTAINS.

MY INFLUENCE WAS ALSO FELT IN THE FIELD OF PSYCHOLOGY THROUGH THE WORK OF MY GODSON, **WILLIAM JAMES**, AUTHOR OF **THE VARIETIES OF RELIGIOUS EXPERIENCE**, **PRAGMATISM**, AND MANY OTHER WORKS.

THE MATCHLESS ELOQUENCE WITH WHICH EMERSON PROCLAIMED THE SOVEREIGNTY OF THE LIVING INDIVIDUAL ELECTRIFIED AND EMANCIPATED HIS GENERATION. POSTERITY WILL RECKON HIM A PROPHET...HIS WORDS ARE CERTAIN TO BE QUOTED MORE AND MORE AS TIME GOES ON, AND TO TAKE THEIR PLACE AMONG THE SCRIPTURES OF HUMANITY.
—WILLIAM JAMES

I **DIED IN 1882**, AT THE AGE OF SEVENTY-EIGHT. ON MY GRAVE MARKER IS A PASSAGE FROM ONE OF MY POEMS. MY VOICE REACHED FAR AND WIDE, AND CONTINUES TO REVERBERATE TO THIS DAY.

RALPH WALDO EMERSON
BORN IN BOSTON MAY 25 1803
DIED IN CONCORD APRIL 27 1882
THE PASSIVE MASTER LENT HIS HAND
TO THE VAST SOUL THAT OER HIM PLANNED

# CREDITS

## PRIMARY SOURCES

The text of this book weaves together passages paraphrased from the following works of Emerson's:

### ESSAYS

"Compensation," from *Essays: First Series*
"Inspiration," from *Letters and Social Aims*
*Nature* (book-length essay)
"The Over-Soul," from *Essays: First Series*
"Self-Reliance," from *Essays: First Series*
"Success," from *Society and Solitude*
"Worship," from *Conduct of Life*

### JOURNAL ENTRIES

December 28, 1826
November 5, 1830
March 4, 1831
September 13, 1831
January 10, 1832
May 26, 1832
July 14, 1832
September 14, 1832
October 1, 1832
September 8, 1833
October 24, 1833

## LECTURES

"The Divinity School Address"
"The Method of Nature"
"The Transcendentalist"
"The Uses of Natural History"

## SERMONS

CXXXIX, on I John 3:20–21
CLI, on Acts 16:28
CXLIII, on Philippians 3:13–14
CXLIV, on Hebrews 6:1
CXLV, on Luke 12:57
CLV, on Mark 8:37
CLVII, on Acts 17:24–25, 29–31
CLIX, on II Corinthians 13:8
CLX, on Colossians 1:9–10
CLXII, on Romans 14:17
CLXIII, on John 3:36
CLXIV, on Ephesians 4:23–24
CLXV, on John 16:13
CLXX, on Colossians 3:2
December 27, 1834
October 19, 1836
November 13, 1838
November 14, 1838

# QUOTES

## TITLE PAGE

"The secret of life"—adapted from Emerson's Journals, December 13, 1826.

## EMERSON AT SEA

Biographical information is from Robert D. Richardson, *Emerson: The Mind on Fire* (University of California Press, 1995).

"That which I cannot yet declare"—Emerson's Journals, September 17, 1833.

"A subtle chain"—Ralph Waldo Emerson, *Nature: Illustrated Edition* (American Renaissance, 2009), epigraph.

## THE IMMENSITY OF THE SOUL

"The mind sees"—Elbert Hubbard, *Elbert Hubbard: A Treasury* (Sam Torode Book Arts, 2016), p. 25.

"The light that shines"—*The Upanishads* (trans. Swami Prabhavananda & Frederick Manchester, Signet Classics, 2002), p. 73.

"The Tao that can be understood"—Lao Tzu, *Tao Te Ching* (trans. Dwight Goddard & Sam Torode, Ancient Renewal, 2019), p. 1.

"When beauty is only"—Lao Tzu, *Tao Te Ching*, p. 2.

"The remark of a child"—Vasistha, *Vasistha's Yoga* (trans. Swami Venkatesanada, SUNY Press, 1993), p. viii.

## 1. TRUST YOURSELF

"There's nothing you can do"—Joseph Campbell, *Pathways to Bliss* (New World Library, 2004), p. 108.

"I would not have"—Henry David Thoreau, *Walden* (American Renaissance, 2009), p. 36.

"You must enter"—Campbell, *Pathways to Bliss*, p. xxvi.

"A mighty tree"—Lao Tzu, *Tao Te Ching*, p. 64.

"If you advance"—adapted from Thoreau, *Walden*, p. 174.

## 2. AS YOU SOW, YOU WILL REAP

"We are not punished for"—Hubbard, *Elbert Hubbard: A Treasury*, p. 43.

"Those who steal"—Lao Tzu, *Tao Te Ching*, p. 81.

"Your life is shaped"—adapted from the Buddha, *Dhammapada* (trans. Eknath Easwaran, Nilgiri Press, 2007), p. 105.

"Fate is nothing"—Vasistha, *Vasistha's Yoga*, p. 28.

## 3. NOTHING OUTSIDE YOU CAN HARM YOU

"Lameness may strike"—Epictetus, *Manual* (trans. Thomas Wentworth Higginson & Sam Torode, Ancient Renewal, 2017), p. 13.

"No one can hurt me"—Marcus Aurelius, *Meditations* (trans. George Long & Sam Torode, Ancient Renewal, 2017), p. 11.

"They may kill me"—Socrates, quoted in Epictetus, p. 60.

## 4. THE UNIVERSE IS INSIDE YOU

"Find tongues in trees"—Shakespeare, *Measure for Measure*, Act II, Scene 1.

"The laws of time and space"—Campbell, *Pathways to Bliss*, p. 106.

"Cosmic consciousness alone"—Vasistha, *Vasistha's Yoga*, p. 52.

"There is Being"—Lao Tzu, *Tao Te Ching*, p. 25.

## 5. IDENTIFY WITH THE INFINITE

"When one is convinced"—Vasistha, *Vasistha's Yoga*, p. 45.

"Think of electric lights"—Joseph Campbell, *Thou Art That* (New World Library, 2001), pp. 20–21.

"If you focus"—Aurelius, *Meditations*, p. 30.

"To those who identify"—adapted from Vasistha, *Vasistha's Yoga*, p. 164.

## 6. LIVE IN THE PRESENT

"The present moment"—Aurelius, *Meditations*, p. 15.

"Eternity is not future"—Campbell, *Pathways to Bliss*, p. 18.

"God culminates in the present"—Thoreau, *Walden*, p. 50.

"The things most people pursue"—Aurelius, *Meditations*, p. 45.

## 7. SEEK GOD WITHIN

"At whose behest"—adapted from *Upanishads*, p. 136.

"What would it profit"—Jesus, Matthew 16:26.

"When Jesus says"—Campbell, *Thou Art That*, p. 19.

"The word unto the prophet"—Emerson, "The Problem, *Poems*.

## EMERSON'S LIFE & INFLUENCE

Biographical information is from Robert D. Richardson, *Emerson: The Mind on Fire*.

On Walt Whitman and Emerson, see:
http://www.state.nj.us/dep/parksandforests/historic/whitman/america.htm

Emily Dickinson, Letter from Dickinson to Otis Phillips Lord, April 30, 1882.

On Emily Dickinson and Emerson, see:
http://edhds11.umwblogs.org/tag/ralph-waldo-emerson

On John Muir and Emerson, see:
https://vault.sierraclub.org/john_muir_exhibit/people/emerson.aspx

William James, "Address to the Emerson Centenary at Concord," *Memories and Studies* (Longmans Green, 1903).

Printed in Poland
by Amazon Fulfillment
Poland Sp. z o.o., Wrocław

59144983R00035